Sir Gawain and the Green Knight

Sir Gawain and the Green Knight

A Comedy for Christmas

Translated from Middle English by
Theodore Silverstein

Illustrated by Virgil Burnett

The University of Chicago Press
Chicago and London

And wener þen Wenore, as þe wyʒe þoʒt

The University of Chicago Press, Chicago 60637
The University of Chicago Press, Ltd., London

CIP data appear on page 122

Contents

I   Outrageous Proposal by a Stranger 1
II   Journey to Another Christmas 25
III   Gawain in Bed and Jeopardy 55
IV   The Glory and the Shame of It 95

O dignitosa coscienza e netta,
Come t'è picciol fallo amaro morso!
O conscience clean and clear, precise and prim,
How bitter seems so small a sin to thee!
Dante, Purgatorio, iii. 8–9

Part I

Once the siege and sack of Troy had ceased—
The bailey breached and burnt to brands and ashes—
The lad who laid the traps of treason there
Was tried for that, the clearest case in town.
Then noble Aeneas it was and his great nation
Who later conquered lands and ruled as lords
Of well-nigh all the wealth of the Western Isles,
As Romulus extends his reach to Rome,
With circumstance establishes that city
And names the name it now is named, his own;
Tirius turns and timbers Tuscan towns;
Longbard lifts up homes in Lombardy;
And far across the French sea Felix Brutus
On many broad-spread banks that British nation builds with
                    pleasure,
            Where war and wrack and wonder
            Have occupied their leisure
            And often bliss and blunder
            Appear in alternate measure.

When Britain thus was built by this great baron
Bold lads bred therein who loved a brawl
And turned up trouble in many troubled times.
More odd events have happened there more often
Than anywhere I know of since that age.
Among the men, however, who molded Britain,
Arthur's called most courtly, I recall,
To whom I turn to tell a true adventure
That some men say is strange and singular,
Extreme among King Arthur's marvels even.
Please listen to this lay a little while,
I'll tell it right away as it's recited in
                              the town;
              A story swift, exciting,
              And faithfully set down
              In true and trusty writing—
              A tale of old renown.

This king held Christmas court in Camelot
With many lovely lords, all likely lads,
The Round Table's band of noble brothers,
Joined in carefree joy and jolly play.
At times the heroes hammered at each other,
Jousting as such gentlemen are wont,
Then came into the court to do the carol.
For round them reigned the revels fifteen days
With all the meat and mirth that men could think of;
Such giddy noise, such glorious-sounding laughter,
Delightful din by day, all night the dance,
That happiness rose high in hall and chamber,
Dukes and dames indulging their desires.
With worldly weal complete they dwelt together,
The most accomplished knights, save Christ himself,
The loveliest ladies who have ever lived,
The comeliest king who ever called a court.
For they were fair in all the flush of lovely youth's
                    first age,
          Fortune's favored kind,
          Their sovereign in fine rage.
          In few courts now you find
          A band of like courage.

While the New Year, newly come, was young
The peers were placed in pairs that day at table.
After Arthur entered with his knights
And chanting of the Mass had ceased in chapel,
The cry was keen of clergy and of court,
Announcing Noël, Noël yet again.
The guests then go about exchanging gifts,
Hold their presents high and hand them out,
Gleefully compare the gifts they get;
Ladies laugh though losers in the game
(A kiss!), no gainer glum, as you may guess.
They made this merry din till dinner time
And when they'd washed, politely sought their places,
The seigniors seated suitably by rank,
Queen Gaynor in a graceful gown among them,
Adorned upon a dais richly draped
With brightest silk, a baldachin above
Of toulouse thin and tapestries from Tarsus,
Worked and woven with a wealth of gems
That princes could approve and silver purchase in
                              that day:
              A handsome-looking woman,
              Her dancing eyes were gray;
              Was any fairer no man
              Might speak the truth and say.

But Arthur would not eat till all were served.
He brimmed with spirits rather like a boy
Who liked to lead his life in lively heart,
Unskilled to stay or sit in one place still,
Young blood and restless brain so busied him.
Besides he had a habit which he held to:
Magnificence denied he take his meal
A festive day like this before he found
The quaint account of some obscure adventure,
Some mighty marvel that he might believe in,
Praising princes, arms, and parlous deeds,
Or someone came to seek a sturdy knight
To joust and join with him in jeopardy,
To offer life for life, each granting each
To live or lose as fortune lent them aid.
Such the courtly king's unchanging custom
At each high feast among his famous fellows in
                              the hall.
            And so with proud demeanor
            He stands there straight and tall,
            That New Year no one keener
            For mirth—or what may fall.

Thus stout King Arthur stands beside the dais,
Talking genially of this and that.
The good Sir Gawain sat by Gaynor's side
And Agravain the Heavy Hand as well,
Both nephews of the king and noted knights.
Above them at the board sat Bishop Baldwin
With Yvain son of Urien next to him.
These dined upon the dais with distinction,
At nearby tables other trusty men.
The starting course was served to sound of trumpets
Brightly hung with banners for the banquet.
And now the noise of drums and noble shrill
Of pipes together raised a piercing clamor,
Holding hearts up high with martial music.
There followed then a flood of costly foods
In steaming plenty on so many plates
'Twas hard to pick a place before the people
Where the silver for the sundry servings could
                     be spread.
        A man'd no more to do
        Than reach, to be well fed;
        Twelve dishes for each two,
        Cold beer and wine rich red.

I say no more about their sumptuous service,
For everyone must know that nothing lacked.
Suddenly a second fanfare sounded,
The signal that a further course was coming,
But scarcely had the sound been stopped to silence,
The first course done and deftly cleared away,
There hales in at the door an awesome creature,
The greatest one on earth, to gauge by height.
From throat to thighs so heavy were his thews,
His loins and limbs so very long and large,
I'd judge he was, as half he seemed, a giant,
And yet I must admit he was a man,
Most marvelous in his might to mount a horse;
Magnificent in back and chest his muscles,
His sides and stomach creditably small,
And following proportion features fairly formed
                    and clean.
        They stared at his complexion,
        The oddest face they'd seen;
        He bore it to perfection,
        But 'twas completely green.

Green the man was grained and green his clothes,
The fitted tunic folded to his figure,
The costly cloak that covered it, whose lining
Was sewed with closely sheared and matching skins
Of matchless *blanc et ner*, the hood to match it
Laid back from his locks along his shoulders.
His hose were held up tight and also green
And curved about his calves without a crease,
The spurs beneath of sheer and shining gold,
And on the fellow's feet, their fine-spun borders
Paneled rich, a pair of pointed shoes.
His vesture, we say verily, was verdant,
The bars along his belt, the brilliant jewels
On his suit and saddle, stitched in silk
And richly rayed in fancy rows and patterns.
To tell of half the trifles would be tiring
Of birds and insects braiding the embroidery
In green beads gay with gold threads gleaming through.
The bit studs and the bosses on the breast gear,
His courser's metal clasps and noble crupper
Were green, as were the stirrups that he stood on,
His saddle and its splendid skirts as well,
Which glowed and gleamed with emerald encrustations.
A matching beast he rides superbly mounted in his
                    saddle,
          A great green horse,
          Which, difficult to handle,
          He curbs with skillful force
          And a green embroidered bridle.

This giant in green was got up with great chic,
His own locks and his horse's high-styled hair.
His flowing tresses fell about his arms
And on his breast a beard just like a bush,
Both together hanging handsomely
In even circle sheared above the elbows,
Like a kingly *cap-à-dos,* which covered
The neck and half his arms beneath their curve.
That mighty horse's mane was much the same,
Curled and combed and clothed with countless knots
Turned with golden threads among the green,
One strand of hair, one strand of gold together.
Tail and forelock too were plaited thus,
And a green and brilliant binding bound the tail
Crowned with costly gems along the dock
And caught up stiff by thongs in crisscross knots,
Where many burnished golden bells lay tinkling.
Such a horse and such a handsome rider
Had never arched the eyebrows of the hall in such
                       gay clothes.
          He seemed as sharp as lightning
          And all there would suppose
          That when it came to fighting
          None could stand his blows.

But he was armed with neither helm nor hauberk,
Armor plate, nor gorget fit for fighting,
No shield or spear designed to strike or thrust,
But in one hand he held a branch of holly,
That grows most green when all the groves are bare,
And in the other hand a huge, great axe,
A cruel tool by any calculation,
The head an ell in length, it was so large,
Its hammered spike of greenish steel and gold,
Its burnished bit a broad one, with an edge
Ground to cut as keenly as a razor.
He held the weapon gravely by a handle
Made of wood and wound about with iron
Engraved in green in nicely wrought designs.
The leather lace that looped up at the head
Was twisted round the shaft to tie it tight
And to the lace was tacked a row of tassels
On buttons brightly green in rich brocade.
Across the hall this horseman held his way,
Rode, disdaining danger, to the dais
With haughty, staring face and hailing no man.
The speech that first he spoke aloud was stern:
"Where," he cried, " 's the ruler of this crowd?
I've mind to meet that warrior, and man to man hold
                            parley."
                 The peers in turn he eyed,
                 Peering at them slowly,
                 Pausing to decide
                 Which was held most highly.

A stir ran through the seats to see the stranger,
Each demanding what the deuce it meant
The caller and his cob could have that color:
As green as grass it seemed and even greener
And gleaming like enamel over gold!
All who stood there stared and pushed up closer,
Wondering what in all the world he wanted.
For they had seen odd things but none like this one,
Murmured, must be magic or illusion.
And so these heroes hedged and gave no answer,
Stayed quite still, astonished at his thunder.
A hush like death descended on the hall,
As if in sudden sleep their talk subsided, yet I
       gather
    It wasn't simply fright,
    But some from manners rather
    Were dumb before that knight
    And left the lead to Arthur.

The king saw this intrusion from the table,
Blandly bowed, for he was never bothered,
Said at once, "Dear sir, I bid you welcome.
I head this house and Arthur is my name.
Please get down and stay with us for dinner,
Then afterwards we'll see to what you want."
"No, so save me Heaven!" said the stranger,
"My errand's not to loiter here at ease.
But, sir, men shout your praises to the skies,
They bruit your castles best and rate your barons
The roughest men who ride about in iron,
The manliest and mightiest of mortals,
Pretty lads to tangle with in tourneys.
Your court, besides, is famed for courtliness.
Now that's what calls me here on this occasion.
Be certain by this holly branch I bear
I come in peace and court no warlike quarrel.
Did I choose to come equipped for fighting,
I've got helm and hauberk both at home,
A sharp-tipped spear that shines, a flashing shield,
And other tools whose trade I think I know.
But since I seek no war my gear is softer,
And if you be as brave as bold men say,
You'll gladly grant the little game I'm asking as
                           my right."
              At once comes Arthur's answer:
              He said, "My dear sir knight,
              If handplay's what you're after
              You'll not here lack a fight."

"No, I'll try no fight; to tell the truth,
Beardless boys are all I see before me.
Were I on my courser, clad in steel,
No man could match me here for lack of might.
But of this court I crave a Christmas game;
It's Yuletide and New Year and you seem keen.
If any in this house thinks he's so hardy,
So rash in blood, so reckless, come what may,
He'd chance exchanging chop for chop with me,
I'll give him this great weapon as a gift,
This heavy axe to handle as he likes,
And take his knock upon my naked neck.
If any's tough enough to try me out,
Let him come here quick and claim this weapon,
I give it up forever, it's all his,
And standing on this floor I'll stand his blow,
Granted you agree to guarantee me play
                              for play.
            Yet I'll give him respite
            A full year and a day.
            Here's the axe, come grasp it.
            Well, friends, what d'ye say?"

Did he strike them dumb at first, then dumber
Now they are, these heroes high and low.
The stranger twisted creaking in the saddle,
Rolled his red-rimmed eyes ferociously,
Lowered his bristling eyebrows, glistening green,
Tilted beard and waited for a taker.
When no one said a syllable he snorted,
Stuck his chest out scornfully and spoke:
"Ho, ho!" he cries, "So this is Arthur's house!
The court whose fame's acclaimed in many kingdoms!
Is this what comes of all your pride and conquests,
Your fierceness and your furor and your bragging?
The Round Table's revels and renown
Dissolve before a single stranger's challenge,
You cower here like cowards from a blow!"
With that he laughed so loud that Arthur flinched,
The blood came flooding through his handsome face, but not
                         from fear.
          There rose a storm of anger
          In him and every peer.
          The king was keen in danger;
          He cried as he came near,

Cried, "By God, dear sir, your game is stupid;
A foolish quest invites a foolish answer.
Your boastful words would scare no one I know.
Just hand your axe to me and, Heaven willing,
I'll yield the boon to you that you request."
The king comes quickly close and holds his hand out,
The horseman gets down firmly on his feet.
Arthur takes the axe and grips the handle,
Swings it bold about him, meaning business.
In all his style the stranger stood unbending,
Higher there than others by a head,
Stood a moment stern and stroked his beard,
Then calmly, with a dry look, loosed his cloak.
To stand up to a stroke no more disturbed him
Than drink a draught of wine would ever dash a duke at
                    dinner.
            Beside the queen Sir Gawain
            Bowed in formal manner,
            "Sire," said to his sovereign,
            "Let me have this encounter."

"If you, my honored lord," he said to Arthur,
"Would bid me from this bench to stand there by you,
  Thus letting me politely leave the table,
  And if my sovereign lady would allow,
  I'd come before your noble court in council.
  To say the truth, it seems to me unseemly
  When such a boon is brought up in your hall
  That you yourself should come so quick to claim it
  While this band of bold men sits about you,
  None with higher courage under Heaven
  Or better fists for fighting, so I feel.
  I know, beside them all, I'm slight and stupid;
  To lose my life, it's plain, would matter little,
  My only import is that you're my uncle,
  My body has no value but your blood.
  And since this foolish game does not befit you
  And I have asked you first, I ought to have it.
  If my plea's not proper, let these peers at once
                        dissent."
                    The court conferred together
                    And with one consent
                    Approved, thus freeing Arthur,
                    Sir Gawain's argument.

Then Arthur granted leave to good Sir Gawain,
Who rose up to his feet, came finely forward,
Knelt before his king and claimed the weapon.
With gracious condescension Arthur gave it,
Raised his arm and asked for Heaven's blessing,
Bade that he be bold in heart and hand;
Then cried, "Be careful, nephew, of your carving,
For serve him right and you'll digest, I reckon,
Any cut that he can serve next Christmas."
Axe in hand, Sir Gawain greets the giant,
Boldly bids him not to be abashed.
The green-clad stranger says in cool response:
"Before proceeding let's recite our compact.
But first, sir knight, I ask to know your name.
No tricks about it, please, if I'm to trust you."
"Agreed," the good knight cries, "my name is Gawain.
I aim this blow whatever be the outcome.
In twelve months' time I'll take a blow from you
With any arm you own and from no other. That's
                              the plan."
                    The stranger says, "Believe me,
                    Sir Gawain, as you can,
                    If anyone's to cleave me
                    I'm glad that you're the man.

20

"By God," the green knight cries, "I'm pleased, Sir Gawain,
  Your famous fist will fetch the blow I've sought!
  You've stated fully and without a flaw
  The compact as I put it to the king,
  Except that you must reassure me, sir,
  That on your word you'll seek me anywhere
  On earth you find me and collect your earnings
  For this day's toil before this titled throng."
"Where'll I seek you? What place?" Gawain asks.
"I don't know where you dwell, by him who made me.
  You're unknown to me, knight, in name and nation.
  Identify yourself and show me surely
  How to track you, I'll contrive to turn up,
  This I swear a solemn oath to do."
"That's enough for me, since it's the New Year,"
  The green knight answers Gawain's gallantry.
"I'll tell you when we've tried our tap together.
  When I've felt your stroke—I hope it's smooth—
  Then I'll produce my name and my address,
  So, careful of our compact, you'll come calling,
  To try a little of my entertainment.
  But if I'm silenced here, then you'll succeed
  In staying home, no further search. And now an end
                    to that!
              Come try the tool, it's deadly.
              Remember, tit for tat."
              Cries Gawain, "Sir, quite gladly!"
              And gives the blade a pat.

Then on the ground the green knight gets all set,
Bends his head a bit to bare the flesh
And lays his lovely locks across the top
To leave the neck quite naked to the bone.
Sir Gawain fixed his left foot out before him,
Gripped the handle, arched the axe on high,
And let it slice down swiftly on the skin,
Through the stranger's bones, which shattered sharply,
Through fat and flesh, which parted as it fell,
Until the bit, grim iron, bit the ground.
The stylish head fell severed from the shoulders
And as it bounced about, some booted it.
The gore streamed down the trunk and stained the green.
The stranger did not sway or stop for that
But stoutly stalked ahead on steady legs,
Reached out roughly where the crowd were rooted,
Got his handsome head and heaved it up,
Turned back to his steed and took the reins,
Then stepping on the stirrup swung aloft
And held the head, its hair twined in his hands.
So he sat serenely in his saddle,
Heedless, as it were, of being headless in
                                    that place.
              He thrust his bulk about,
              A horror without face.
              It put the peers in doubt
              Till he recalled his case.

He holds the head up in his hand, head high,
Twists the face to face the princes' table.
Lifting up its lids it stared unblinking,
Licked its lips and spoke aloud like this:
"Gawain, prove that you're prepared as promised
Faithfully to fare until you find me
And hold what here you've sworn in these knights' hearing.
Choose the way, I charge, to the Green Chapel
To liquidate the loan you've lent—you've earned it!
I'll promptly pay in person New Year's Day.
As Knight of the Green Chapel many know me,
So if you try to trail me you won't trifle.
Come or you'll be clearly called delinquent."
He gave a roar and reined his horse around
And haled out at the hall door, head in hand,
As sparks flew sharply from his horse's shoes.
He nipped off, to what nook no man there knew
Any more than whence he haled. What had he led them
                  into?
        The stout King Arthur laughed
        And Gawain gave his grin, too.
        The court all called it daft,
        The maddest play they'd been to.

The courtly king, although he felt some qualms,
Let no hint escape but said aloud,
Politely looking at his lovely consort:
✻ "Dear madam, may no man today dismay you;
Plays like this are part of Christmas parties,
Interludes with lyrics and with laughter,
Between the lords' and ladies' rounds of dancing.
In any case, now I may eat my dinner,
Having seen the sight I can't dispense with."
Then glancing at Sir Gawain he said grandly,
"Hang your axe up now, it's hewn enough, sir."
And it was hung to decorate a hanging
On the wall, where everyone might wonder
Who saw it and recite the story of it.
Together then they bent to meat, these barons,
King and courtly knight, and keen men served them
The finest food on earth in festive helpings.
With every sort of meat and mirth and music
They whiled away the day in weal until the fall
                    of night.
            And now, Sir Gawain, ponder:
            Shall you refrain, in fright,
            From wandering out yonder
            To find and face that knight?

Part II

Arthur had this earnest of adventure,
The season young, his sense for exploits strong,
Yet as they turned to dine his tongue was silent,
For now the game they'd got on hand was grim.
Pleased though Gawain was to start those pastimes,
It should not shock us if the jest end sadly:
Though men be merry in mood when they've drunk deep,
A year runs yare and seldom yields the like,
Commencement scarcely comprehends the close.
Now the Yule ran by and now the New Year
And every season trod upon the other.
After Christmas came the crabbed Lent,
That tries the flesh with fish and simpler food.
The weather of the world then spars with winter,
The cold unclasps the clay, the clouds lift upwards,
The glistening rain descends in warming showers
And falls on fields. The flowers show their faces,
Ground and groves put on their dress of green,
And birds make haste to build and boldly sing,
Joyous at the gentle summer's journey to
                         the hills.
          The blossoms burst and bloom,
          Riotous by the rills;
          Now sounds the springtime's tune
          In lovely woodland trills.

Now spreads the summer with its quiet breezes,
When Zephyr sighs and whispers to the seeds.
Happy is the herb who holds her head up,
When drenching dew has dripped down from her leaves,
To bask beneath the sunshine's blissful glow.
But harvest time comes hastening, soon grows harsh,
And warns her to grow ripe before the winter,
Who down his dry breath drives the dust before him
And blows it fiercely far off from the fields.
On high the wind makes war against the sun,
The leaves pull loose and light upon the ground,
The grass turns gray that formerly was green,
And all that once rose fresh grows old and rots.
And winter, so this whirling world requires as
      we know,
   Returns at Michael's moon
   And brings its wage of woe.
   Now Gawain must face soon
   The hard road he's to go.

With Arthur still he lingers till All Hallows,
Celebrating for his sovereign's sake
The Round Table's rich and varied revels.
Courtly knights and comely ladies both
Were moved to mourning for the man they loved—
Yet showed no sign of any state but mirth;
They joined that knight in jesting without joy.
Then after table, troubled, Gawain talks
With candor to the king about the quest:
"Allow me now, my liege, to leave your presence.
What this case will cost is clear, no reason
To tell you twice the details, just this trifle:
Tomorrow's when I set out on my search
To find our guest in green, as God may guide me,
And bear his blow all bare upon my bones."
Then all the peerless peers appeared together,
Eric and Yvain and others also:
Sir Dodinal Sauvage, the Duke of Clarence,
Lancelot and Lyonel, good Lucan,
Sir Bors as well and Bedivere, both big men,
And other mighty lords, among them Mador.
They came, this courtly circle, near the king,
Called by care to council with the knight.
Throughout the hall there hovered high regret
That one as good as Gawain was should go
To stand a savage stroke and so himself to strike
                              no more.
              The knight said cheerfully,
              "Why should I now despair?
              Our destinies harsh and high
              What can we do but dare?"

He dwells there all that day, at dawn arises,
Asks them for his arms, and all are brought.
First a crimson carpet clothes the pavement,
On which there glitters gilded gear enough.
The stout knight steps on it, assumes the armor,
Dressed up in a richly diapered doublet
Covered by a well-cut *cap-à-dos*
That's fastened firm and finely lined with fur.
They fit the sabatons upon his feet,
His legs are laced in greaves of lightest steel,
With polains, polished bright, appended to them
Knotted round his knees with knots of gold,
Then clever cuisses that with craft enclosed
His thick-set thighs and fastened there with thongs,
Next the burnie bright with burnished links
About his body over lovely lining,
Then shining bracers bound about both arms
With good, gay elbow guards and gloves of plate,
And all the handsome harness that should help him on
                    his ride;
          His surcoat richly braided,
          His golden spurs well tied,
          With silken ceinture girded,
          A sure sword by his side.

When he stood in steel his arms were splendid,
The slightest loop or latchet bright with gold.
Thus harnessed as he is he hears the Mass,
Prays and pays his homage at the altar, ✘
Comes then to the king and to the courtiers,
Politely takes his leave of lords and ladies,
Who kiss him and escort him to the courtyard,
Carefully commending him to Christ.
Gringolet stood groomed nearby and girded,
His saddle gleaming gay with golden fringes
And newly nailed with studs as need required,
The bridle bound about with golden bands,
The setting of the splendid skirts and breast gear,
The crupper and the saddle cloth and bows,
Arrayed alike in red with golden rivets
That glowed and gleamed and glittered like the sun.
Then lightly kissing it he lifts his helmet,
Stapled strong and softly lined inside.
High upon his head and hooked behind
It sat, with shining streamer on the neck guard
Bound and braided with the best of gems
On broad and silken borders, birds between
Like painted popinjays and periwinkles
With turtledoves, and true loves stitched as thick
As if a score of maids had sewed them seven years
                    in town;
            The circlet even richer
            That circumscribed his crown,
            Of perfect diamonds which were
            Both sparkling bright and brown.

They brought him out his shield of brilliant crimson,
A pentacle in pure gold painted on it.
He slung it round his shoulder by the baldric
Where, handsome, it enhanced our hero's image.
The pentacle was perfect for that prince
And why, I stop to tell though it detain me:
For it's a figure that affects five points,
Its lines all interlocking with each other
And endless everywhere, and hence the English
Name it, as I note, the endless knot.
It suited him and his distinguished arms,
For faithful five ways, each in five-fold fashion,
Was Gawain's way, each good and fined like gold,
Freed of every flaw and filled with courtly
                    quality;
            The pentacle wrought new
            On shield and broidery,
            A knight whose words ring true
            And true gentility.

First, in his five senses he's found faultless;
Next, he never failed in his five fingers;
And all his faith on earth was in the five wounds
Of Christ upon the cross, as Creed recounts;
And wherever he was hemmed in battle
His thought throughout was that above all things
His force was founded firmly on the five joys
Our comely Heaven's queen had of her child.
Aptly hence he had her image painted
Inside the inner surface of his shield
Where when he looked his courage never languished.
The fifth of all the fives affected by him
Were fellowship and full free-heartedness,
A cleanliness and courtesy both constant,
A pity that surpassed his other points—
All five of these more firmly fixed within him
Than in any other knight at arms.
These five conjunctures joined within our hero,
Each conjoined to each without an end
And fixed upon five points that never finished,
Nor settled on one side nor came asunder,
Endless everywhere from any angle,
Wherever one might start or one might stop.
And so upon his shield they set the symbol
Royally in ruddy gold on red—
The pentacle as pointed out by people proved and
clever.
Sir Gawain lifts his lance,
Now armed for his endeavor,
Salutes them with his glance
And rides away forever.

He spurred his steed and sprang upon his way
So sharply that the sparks struck sharp behind.
All sighed who saw it, truly sad at heart,
Together talking to each other plainly
For grief, now Gawain's gone. "By Christ, it's grievous
That, lord, you shall be lost who lived so nobly!
To light again upon his like's not likely.
Wiser to have worked more warily
And made that modest man a mighty duke.
In our land to be a brilliant leader
Of men, is more his mark than be beheaded
By an elvish man for our vainglory.
Who ever knew a king to court such counsel
As place a knight for Christmas play in peril!"
Water welled up warm in weeping eyelids
As our hero left behind familiar haunts
                              that day.
            He would not wait at home
            But quickly went his way.
            Endless roads he'd roam,
            As my source would say.

Through the realm of Logres rides our hero
Gawain, and, by God, it seems no game
To him; he often spends the night alone
And fails to find the fare before him tasty.
He counts no comrade other than his courser
Crossing fields and fells, and has no friend
But God to talk to. Thus he travels on
Until he comes in close to northern Wales
And holding left the isles round Anglesey,
Crosses by the fords below the forelands
To Holyhead and hence attains by land
The Wilderness of Wirral, where men wander
Who love with good heart neither God nor men.
As he rode he asked of all he met there,
Had they heard of any nearby chapel,
Green and guarded by an all-green knight?
They shook their heads and said they'd never seen
A chap all covered up in any color like
                    that quite.
          Many a twisting byway
          Was taken by our knight,
          His heart turned this and that way,
          Before he found the site.

Many cliffs he climbed in distant countries,
Faring far from friends, a friendless stranger.
At every creek or crossing that he came to
He found a foe—if not it was a wonder—
And him so foul and fell he had to fight him.
He sees so many marvels in the mountains,
'Twould be hard to tell the tenth part of them.
At times he wars with dragons and with wolves,
With wasteland trolls who dwell among the scree,
At other times with bulls and bears and boars
And giants who hunt him from the jutting crags.
Had he not been doughty and enduring,
(Undeviating, dutiful to God,
He often doubtless had been done to death.
Yet war did not so wound him but that winter
Was worse. The clouds shed water clear and cold,
Which froze before it touched the faded earth.
He slept, half dead from sleet, in his cold steel
Through nights enough among the naked rocks,
Where clattering from the crest the cold stream runs
And hangs hard icicles above his head.
Thus in peril and pain and grievous plight
This knight rides on till Christmas Eve, across the land
                              alone.
          To Mary in that season
          He gravely made his moan,
          Asking that he see soon
          The way to some poor home.

Among the hills he moves next morning bravely,
Deep into a wild and heavy woodland,
On either side high slopes and down beside them
A hundred huge and hoary oaks together,
The hazel and the hawthorn all entangled,
Rough and ragged moss spread everywhere,
And birds, dejected, perched on bare-swept branches,
Piteously peeping for the cold.
Gringolet's good master glides beneath them
Through many a mire and bog, a man alone,
Filled with fear lest he should fail to find
A service for the Sire whom that same night
A Maid bore to amend our maladies.
So sighing he said, "I beseech thee, Lord,
And Mary, gentle Mother dear to me,
Some haven to devoutly hear the Mass in
And tomorrow's matins, I ask meekly.
Hence I repeat in prayer my Pater, Ave, and
                    my Creed."
            Riding as he prayed,
            He wept for each misdeed,
            Signed himself and said,
        "May Christ's cross grant me speed."

Hardly had he hallowed himself three times
When he was aware within the wood
Of a moated dwelling on a meadow
Above a glade and set about with branches
From many mighty trunks along the margins;
The noblest castle any knight could have,
Pitched upon a lawn within a parkland
Stoutly pent up by a pointed paling
That took in countless trees for more than two miles.
This side our hero scrutinized the stronghold
As it shone and shimmered through the shining
Oaks. He doffed his helm, gave humble thanks
To Jesus and Saint Julian, gentlemen
Who'd heard his call and showed this courtesy.
"Now comfortable quarters," quoth the knight,
"Please grant." His golden heels goad Gringolet,
Who chooses by pure chance the chief approach
And carries thus our champion coursing to the bridge
                                in haste.
                    But it was hauled up hard,
                    The gates were fastened fast,
                    The walls stood firm on guard,
                    Defying winter's blast.

The knight clung to his steed, which pulled up short
Upon the bank above a broad and deep
Double ditch that dammed the castle in.
The walls were deeply set within the water,
Out of which they rose to ample heights
In rough-hewn ranks that reached the cornices,
Where horizontal courses capped them clean
Above the moldings by the battlements,
In keeping with the mason's classic precepts.
At intervals were turrets gaily topped,
With handsome loopholes that could lock up tight.
A better barbican he'd never seen.
He eyed the high-built hall within the curtain
Set with towers, turrets thick upon them
Fitted out with fancy finials,
Very slender, capped by skillful carvings;
And on the roofs a chain of chalk-white chimneys
Winked all white above the castle walls.
So many painted pinnacles pointed skyward,
Embrasures clustered so about the keep,
It called to mind a complex paper cutout.
The knight believed the castle fine enough,
Could he only come within its close.
To linger in that lodging for the season would be
                              pleasant.
                    Quickly, as he calls,
                    A porter asks his errand,
                    Smiling from the walls
                    And greeting our knight-errant.

Sir Gawain cries, "Please carry my request
For lodging to this lofty castle's lord."
"Yea, Peter," pipes the porter, "it's my pleasure
To welcome you to stay, sir, while you wish,"
Then turns away at once, as soon returns
With servants ready to receive the stranger.
They get the great bridge down, go out, and kneeling
On the frozen earth upon their knees,
Greet the guest with grace as he deserves.
They wind the broad gate wide, make way for him,
He bids them rise and rides across the bridge
Where stout men hold his saddle as he dismounts
And others stoutly lead his steed to stable.
Knights and squires then come smiling down
To hale our hero to the hall with joy.
As he unhinged his helmet many hands
Reached out to lift it from his hands to help him,
And they assumed, besides, his sword and shield.
Then he greeted each knight graciously
And many proud men pressed to pay him honor.
They brought him, buckled in steel, within the hall,
Where on the hearth a lovely fire burned high.
Their lord without delay then leaves his chamber
Politely to receive his guest below.
"You're welcome to whatever here you wish,"
He says, "it's all your own to have and hold with my
                                        accord."
            "I thank you," says the knight,
            "Christ grant you your reward."
              Then host and guest, moved quite,
              Embrace with warm regard.

comradarie between nobles

Gawain marked the man who made him welcome
And owned him apt as owner of the castle,
A knight, in fact, enormous, in his prime,
Stern, erect and stout on stalwart legs—
Broad and bright his beard and brown as beaver,
Face as fierce as fire and his voice
Commanding—just the man, our knight admits,
For lordship of good lieges in a castle.
The lord conducts him duly to a chamber,
Commands a man be sent at once to serve him.
Knights enough were nimble at his nod
To seek the bedroom bright with noble bedding,
Silken curtains sheer with clear gold stitching
And covers covered skillfully with fur
Of brilliant *blanc et ner* and bright embroidery,
Runners hung on ropes, their rings red gold,
And on the walls from Toulouse and from Tarsus
Red carpets, rugs in keeping on the floor.
There they stripped him with good-natured speeches,
The burnie from his back, his burnished harness,
And in their place brought proud robes to him promptly
To try, exchange and choose among the choicest.
As soon as he had picked and put one on him
Whose flowing skirts sat well upon his figure,
It seemed, from his new semblance, like the spring
To nearly all the knights who saw him now,
The colors glowing lovely on his limbs.
No finer knight could Christ have ever fashioned, so
                              they thought.
                    Wherever was his home,
                    It seemed as if he ought
                    To stand, a prince alone,
                    In fields where proud men fought.

42

A chair before the hearth where charcoal burned
Was comfortably covered for Sir Gawain
With quilted coverlets and costly cushions;
A splendid robe was cast about his shoulders
Of rich embroidered wool both bright and warm,
And finely lined inside with finest fur,
Ermine all of it, his hood the same.
In luxury he settled in that settle,
Warmed himself and soon his spirits rose.
A table then was set upon its trestles,
Covered with a cloth of shining white,
With serviettes and salts and silver spoons.
Our warrior washed his hands and went to table,
The servants served him swift and skillfully
With sundry broths and stews, superbly seasoned,
A double fill, in fact, of many fishes,
Some baked in bread, some broiled upon the coals,
Some boiled, some served as stew and seethed with spices,
And also sauces subtle on his palate.
Frequently he called the food a feast;
Men urged him on with grace, with grace he heeded what
                              they said:
          " 'Tis penance now you're taking,
            You'll soon be better fed!"
          Grew merry at their joking
          As wine went to his head.

Then tactfully they tried to prompt the prince
Of his courtesy, by covert questions,
To concede he came from that same court
Which Arthur, king of courtesy, then kept,
The royal ruler of the Table Round,
And he himself was Gawain sitting there,
Come to them at Christmas by pure chance.
So when the lord had learned whom he had lured there,
Loud he laughed, he thought it so delightful,
And in that place the men took pleasure promptly
To turn up in his presence at that time,
Observe his person's strength and quality,
His purity of manners, and to praise them;
Before all men on earth his fame is fairest.
Each man whispered to the one beside him,
"Now we'll know sophisticated conduct
And unexceptionable knightly speech;
We'll learn just how to do it without asking,
For here we've got the father of fine manners.
Of his goodness God thus grants his grace
Who gives us such a goodly guest as Gawain.
And good men glad of Gawain's birth shall sit and sing
                            and lark.
                    The meaning of good manners
                    This man shall make us mark.
                    I'm sure we'll be the gainers
                    For learning lovers' talk."

44

By the time of day when, dinner done,
The knight arose, the night was nearly falling.
Chaplains crossed the courtyard to the chapels
And rang the richly rounded peals of bells
The sacred season's evensong required them.
The lord attends the service and the lady
Appears as well, but with propriety
Passes to a pretty, private pew.
Gaily clothed, Sir Gawain comes in shortly.
His host takes up his mantle by a fold
And, naming him by name familiarly,
Steers him to a seat, the same time saying
He's the one of all the world most welcome.
Sir Gawain blessed him and they both embraced
And sat together gravely through the service.
The lady pleased to look then on the knight
And came out of her comely pew's seclusion,
A daintiness of damsels drawn about her.
Fairest was she in her form and body,
Her skin, her cheeks, her color and her movement,
Surpassing all the others, and indeed
Gainlier than Gaynor, Gawain thought.
She moved to meet him, moving through the chancel.
On her left another lady led her,
Older sure than she, indeed a senior
To whom the knights about her owned respect.
Both these ladies were unlike to look at:
Where one was fresh, the other one was withered;
Cheeks glowed rich and red upon the one,
The other's fell in rough and wrinkled folds.
Kerchiefs on the one, pure white with pearls,
Displayed her bosom and her bare white throat,
Which shone like snow that shimmers on the hills;

The other had a gorget on her neck,
Her swarthy chin confined by chalk-white veils,
Her forehead frilled and folded so in silk,
Embroidered and embarrassed by such trifles,
That nothing did she bare but black-arched eyebrows,
Naked lips and nose and both her eyes,
The last two sour to see, all sore and bleary.
A noble dame on earth may men announce her in
                              God's name!
                    Her body short and heavy,
                    Her buttocks broad in frame;
                    More luscious in that bevy
                    The one led by this dame!

When Gawain glimpsed that girl who looked so gracious
He went to meet them with the lord's permission.
The elder he salutes in low obeisance,
The fairer folds a little in his arms
And kisses gently, greeting them with grace.
They beg to know him better and he brightly
Sues to be their servant, if it suit them.
He turns between them, talking, to his chamber,
To the chimney corner, where they call
For spice cakes, which the servants swiftly bring
In heaps, and honeyed wine to every bite.
His lordship danced about in little leaps,
Reminding them that all must make quite merry,
Took his hood and hung it on a spear
And urged them each to win the honor of it,
Whoever made most mirth that Christmastime—
"With friendly aid I aim to try my own hand
Before, in faith, I forfeit any finery!"
The lord thus with his laughter makes things lively
To entertain Sir Gawain in the hall with games
                              that night,
              Until there comes the moment
              The lord can call for light
              And guest bow his retirement
              To bed for some respite.

In the morning as each man remembers
How the Lord was led to death to save us,
In every cot and castle in the world
For his sake burgeons joy. So it did here
On this day with a thousand pleasantries.
On sideboards and at service on the dais
Servants set a sumptuous cuisine.
At the table's head the ancient dame
Is seated with all honor by the host,
Who entertains her with, I trust, complaisance.
Gawain and the gay wife dine together
Meetly near the middle of the table,
The others as seems best throughout the hall.
When every sir was settled suitably
Meat was there, there mirth, there much rejoicing:
'Twould gravel me to give a good account of it,
Should I try perhaps to tell its details.
Yet our knight, I know, and lady fair
Found such pleasure in each other's presence—
Their dainty dalliance and *double entendre*,
But pure, refined and free from lewd suggestion—
Their play surpassed the play of any princes, I
                              dare say.
                    The pipes then pipe out shrill,
                    Drums beat, trumpets bray,
                    And each man eats his fill
                    As likewise so do they.

Pleasure thrives on that day and the next,
The third day, just as happy, hurries after,
For on Saint John's the games sound gay indeed;
Then follows Innocents' with song and laughter,
The last, they think, of that year's celebrations.
There are guests to go at morning's gray,
And so they wait up wide-eyed, drinking wine,
And dance their favorite carols dauntlessly.
At last, when it was late, they took their leave
For each to wend his way who dwelt a distance.
Gawain says goodbye to them, his good host
Takes his arm and leads him to his own haunts,
Draws him to the fire there, thanks him deeply
For the signal deference he has shown him
In honoring his house at this high season
And brightening up this castle with his *belle chère.*
"Be bound, sir, while I live, I'll be the better
  That Gawain's been my guest at God's own birthday."
"In good faith," Gawain says, "sir, though I'm grateful,
  The honor is your own, it's all your doing,
For which the one on high grant you reward.
For me, I'm moved to do as you admonish,
Which is my obligation here in all things, if
                    I may."
              The lord then cast his net
              To make Sir Gawain stay.
              The knight expressed regret
              That he could see no way.

The host politely asked our hero then
What solemn business had, that special season,
Called him from the king's court all alone
Before they'd haled the holly out of town.
"In truth, sir," says the knight, "you say what's true.
A task both grave and pressing took me thence,
Which summons me to seek out such a place
As I myself have not the slightest notion
Where to wander in the world to find it.
I'm doubtful I can reach it New Year's Day
For all the land in Logres, Lord so help me!
Therefore I, sir, ask you here this question:
Tell me truly have they told you tales of
The Green Chapel and the ground it stands on
And the knight, in green as well, who guards it?
We devised by voice a vow between us
To meet there at that mark, if I survived.
Little time is left before this New Year
And I'd rather, if God would arrange it,
Find that fellow than possess a fortune!
Hence, with your agreement, I must go,
Since now I've barely three days to get busy;
I'd just as freely fall as fail my mission."
With laughter cries the lord, "Then you can linger,
For I shall get you to your goal in good time.
The Green Chapel's site no more need grieve you.
But you shall lie in bed, sir, until late,
Defer until the first day of the year
Your going, yet you'll gain your goal by noon and do
your part.
Stay till New Year's Day
And then rise up and start.
We'll set you on your way,
We're not two miles apart."

Gawain then was glad and gaily laughed.
"For this above all other things, my thanks.
And now my quest's achieved, at your request
I'll stay and do whatever else you ask."
His lordship seized him, sat him down beside him,
Called the ladies to enlarge their pleasure.
They savored this decision by themselves,
The host so taken up with happy talk,
A man beside himself for sheer affection,
He hardly knew for joy what next to do.
Then crying loud he calls out to the knight,
"You've offered to perform what I shall ask;
Will you keep this promise here at once?"
"I will so, sir," our trusty hero says,
"For while I stay with you I'm at your service."
Says the lord, "You've labored riding long,
And since stayed up with me; you're not yet strengthened
Enough by sleep and nourishment, I know.
So you shall lie in bed at leisure late
Tomorrow morning, come down for your meal
Just when you wish, my wife will wait for you
And keep you company till I come back. And while you're
                                        resting
            I'll rise and rouse my horse
            And early go out hunting."
            Sir Gawain cries of course,
            With simple grace assenting.

"Let's add another compact," cries our host.
"My winnings in the wood shall go to you,
  What here you get you'll give me in exchange.
  Now swear in truth, good sir, we'll make that swap,
  However it turns out, for worse or better."
"By God," cries good Sir Gawain, "I agree!
  It pleases me that you're disposed to play."
"If someone brings a drink we'll bind the bargain,"
  Laughed the castle's lord, and each one laughing
  Drank and joked and dallied merrily.
  These lords and ladies happy in their leisure,
  Full of fancy chaffer in French fashion,
  Stood exchanging small talk intimately
  Until they kissed their courteous adieus.
  With servants bearing bright and blazing torches
  Lord and knight, each one, was led that night to his
                    soft bed,
          And as he fell asleep
          The compact filled his head:
          The old lord of the keep
          Would keep the terms as said.

Part III

Well before the day they woke up early.
The guests who plan to go rouse out their grooms
And swiftly see their steeds are saddled up,
Get their gear together, pack their bags,
Dress to ride arrayed to show their rank,
Leap up lively, lightly take the reins,
And each one makes his way to where he's bound.
The land's obliging lord was not the last
Arrayed for riding, with his rich attendance.
He heard the Mass and had a hasty snack
And as the daylight dimly dawned he sat
Among his henchmen high upon his horse.
Huntsmen who knew how then coupled the hounds,
Unclosed the kennel doors and called them out,
Blew three single blasts upon the bugles,
At which the brachets bayed a lovely bellow.
A hundred well-trained huntsmen, as I heard,
Whip them in and win back every one that runs
                              astray.
                    To post the keepers go
                    And loose their hounds away,
                    And soon the bugles' blow
                    Disturbs the woodland way.

The baying once begun, the wild beasts trembled;
Deer drove through the dales, half dazed with fear,
Hastened to the high ground but were headlong
Beaten back by beaters, who cried boldly.
They let the harts through with their lofty heads,
The brave bucks also with their broad flat antlers:
The noble lord forbade that in closed season
Any man might menace any male deer.
The hinds were hemmed in with a Hey! and a 'Ware!
With din the does were driven to the valleys;
As they scatter see the slant of arrows—
From every woodland winding whizzed a missile—
Whose broad and big heads bit the brown hides deeply.
So! They bray and bleed and die upon the banks,
The hounds pursue the scent unceasingly,
And hunters hasten after them with horns
And such a cracking cry would crack a cliff.
The animals escaping from the arrows
Were trapped and torn at stations set to take them,
Driven down the daleside to the waters.
The lower station keepers were so skilled,
The greyhounds were so great, they got them quickly
And slaughtered them as swiftly as they bounded
                              into sight.
              The lord laughed like a boy,
              Both mounted and alight,
              Driven all day by joy
              Until the fall of night.

The lord thus plies his pleasure in the woodlands
While Gawain lies at leisure in his bed,
Snugly as the sun slants down the walls,
Curtained round, beneath a costly cover.
And as he slumbered softly he discerned
A scratch upon his door, which slyly opened.
At once he heaves his head up from the bedclothes,
Lifts the curtain lightly by the corner
And wary waits to see who it may be.
It was the lady looking very lovely,
Who quickly closed the quiet door behind her
And reached his couch. Our cavalier blushed crimson,
Sank back softly, breathed as if asleep.
She made no sound but tip-toed to his side,
Caught the curtain up and crept beneath it,
Softly set herself beside the bed
And waited all the while for him to waken.
Our hero lay there lurking very long,
Weighing what this watchful waiting meant,
This intimate incursion's consequence.
He then said to himself, " 'Twould be more seemly
At once to ask her openly her errand,"
Pretended waking, stretched and turned to her,
Opened up his eyes as if surprised,
Crossed himself and just to be secure he said
                    a prayer.
          Sweet her chin and cheeks,
          In color pink and fair;
          With lovely lips she speaks,
          Her laugh as light as air.

"Good morning, Gawain," gaily said the lady,
"You sleep so sound a lass can slip in easy.
  You're caught at once! Unless we make a compact
  I'll bind you in your bed, you may be bound."
  These shafts the lady launched with merry laughter.
"Good morning, charmer," blithely cries Sir Gawain,
"I'm pleased to put myself at your disposal.
  I bend abject at once and ask your mercy;
  When fall one must, 'tis folly to defy."
  He thus responds with pretty repartee.
"But, lovely lady, if you'd lend your leave,
  And loose your captive's links and let him rise,
  I'd leave this bed and be the better bound
  To fashion further pleasures for this parley."
"Oh, not at all, *beau sire*," she answered sweetly,
"You shan't get up, I see a surer plan:
  I'll fasten you more firmly, hand and foot,
  And then discuss conditions with my captive.
  For I can guess that you're the great Sir Gawain,
  To whom the world pays homage everywhere.
  The *beau monde* rate your manners and your morals
  As nice as any gentleman's now alive.
  My husband and his henchmen all have gone,
  The servants and the maids are all asleep,
  The door is closed, its lock securely fastened.
  Since here I've him whom all delight to honor,
  I'd love to learn the loving ways allowed us by this
                          moment.
              My body's yours in fee,
              Impose whatever payment;
              In pure propriety
              I am, dear sir, your servant."

"In faith," Sir Gawain says, "I feel quite flattered,
  Though not the paragon whom you depict.
  I'm well aware how utterly unworthy
  I am to have such honor as you offer.
  By Heaven, I'd be happy, if you asked it,
  To suit your every sigh with courtly service,
  To teach with gentle talk would be pure joy."
"In truth, dear sir," returns the lady brightly,
"If the dash and style which dazzle others
  Relaxed or lost their edge they'd lose their charm.
  How many ladies now alive would rather
  Have you, kind sir, as now I have you here,
  Hanging sweetly on your loving speech
  And seeking comfort to assuage their care,
  Than all the shining silver they possess!
  But I too love that lord who lights our heaven,
  I hold him in my hands whom all desire, by
                          happy chance."
                  She played to him so brightly
                  And charmed him by her glance;
                  The knight with words turned lightly
                  Countered each advance.

"May Mary," says he merry, "mark you, madam.
  I find your generous offer fine, believe me.
  Too frequently the others follow fashion,
  Treating me beyond my true attainments;
  But your respect displays your special nature."
"By Mary," she, "I'd say its source lies elsewhere.
  Could I enwind in me all women's worth
  And have the wealth of all the world in fee,
  And should I bid and bargain for a husband,
  For virtues such as I've divined in you—
  Manly beauty, grace, a friendly manner—
  Which, formerly alleged, I find confirmed,
  None on earth should get the nod before you."
"But, ma'am," he says, "you've married well already.
  I'm proud, though, of the price you put upon me.
  Your servant, I here take you for my sovereign.
  I now become your knight, may Christ be kind."
  As morning passed they talked of many things,
  The lady bold as if she loved him dearly,
  The gallant knight engaged in his defense.
"The fairer face," the thoughtful dame reflected,
"The less the love. He'll lightly dodge the danger, if
                    he may,
          Of battle in this war,
          He's forced to fight that way."
          She asks then to withdraw;
          He grants it right away.

She said goodbye and laughed, then at a glance
 Loosed a shaft from where she stood that shook him:
"The Warder of all words reward your work,
 It comes to me you cannot be Sir Gawain."
"Why not?" he cries, the question quick for fear
 He'd failed in some refinement of locution.
 She says, "God see you," then asserts her reason:
"A man as fine as Gawain's felt to be,
 Who makes himself a mirror of good manners,
 Could not linger easily with a lady
 And not request a kiss from courtesy,
 Trusting to some trifling turn of phrase."
"Then let it be," laughs Gawain, "as you like,
 To kiss at your command becomes a knight.
 No pleasure to displease you, plead no more."
 She came quite close and caught him in her arms,
 Inclining to the couch with grace to kiss him.
 They charmingly commend them each to Christ,
 And out she slips without a further sound.
 He rises and gets ready quick to dress,
 Calls his body servant, picks his clothes,
 And when he's groomed he gaily goes to Mass.
 He went then to a worthy meal laid waiting,
 Passed the day in pleasantries till moonrise with
                           great zest.
              No likelier ladies ever
              Have entertained a guest,
              The old and young together,
              With happy tale and jest.

Still the country's lord pursues his sport,
Hunting fawnless hinds through holt and heath.
Such a kill of does and other deer
He scored by sundown, it was past assessing.
Then gallantly they gathered in the gloaming
And quickly got the fallen game together.
Knights of noblest rank and men enough
Pick the fullest fleshed that they can find
And break them with a beautiful precision
According to the canons of that craft.
Of those they try there at the first assay
The thinnest tests of fat two fingers thick.
They slit the breast of each and seize the gullet,
Scrape it with a knife and knot it neatly,
Trim the four legs then and tear the hide off,
Break the belly, bring the bowels out
With care in case the knot should come undone.
They grasp the gorge and gracefully dissect
The wizzen from the windpipe, fling the guts out,
Sharp knives shear the shoulders off and draw them
Through a little hole to leave whole sides.
Now they break the breast up in two pieces,
Turn back to the gorge and tend to it,
Swiftly slit it straight down to the forelegs,
Remove the muscles of the neck, the membranes
By the ribs then rip out rapidly;
Cut across correctly by the hipbones,
Hew down to the haunches that adjoin them
And lift them up and hack them off all whole.
And that they name the numbles, as I know the
                              gamebooks do.
                    Where the hind legs meet
                    They cut the skin folds through
                    And then, to free the meat,
                    Along the backbone hew.

The head and neck they hack away and after
Quickly cut the flanks off from the chine
And throw the "ravens' fee" into a thicket.
Near the ribs they hole both heavy flanks through
And hang them, each one separate, by the hocks
So every man can have the share that's his.
Upon the creatures' hides they feed the hounds,
Giving them the livers, lights and tripes
And bread all bathed in blood and mixed together.
They boldly blow the *prise* and bay their hounds,
Take their portions, turn again toward home,
Stoutly sounding many mighty motes.
The day was done, at dark they reached at last
The cheerful castle, where at ease our cavalier
                              remained,
                    A fire before him set,
                    Which now the lord regained,
                    And as the two there met
                    Their joy was unrestrained.

Our host then has the household brought together,
Calls both ladies with their damsels down
Before the host assembled in the hall.
He bids men bring his venison before him
And gaily hales Sir Gawain to his side,
Tallies up the tails of tall-grown creatures,
Shows the shorn white flesh inside the ribs.
"How d'ye like this game then? Have I earned
Your praise? And shouldn't my skill deserve some thanks?"
"Indeed," the knight comes back, "this bag's the best
I've seen in seven years at winter season."
"I give it all to you," the host cries, "Gawain,
It's yours to claim in keeping with our compact."
"That's true," our hero cries, "and here's my counter:
What I've won of worth within these walls
I yield to you with equal will as yours."
He puts his arms around the handsome shoulders
And kisses him as courtly as he can.
"There, my taking take, I took no more.
I'd grant it to you gladly were it greater."
"It's good, thanks, as it is," the good host cries,
"And could well count for more because of where
Your tactics took it, if you'd only tell me."
"No, that's not our compact, no more questions,"
Says our knight, "You've got your share, to seek for more's
                        not fair."
                    They laugh and think that clever,
                    Their jesting fills the air,
                    And so to sup together
                    On dainties rich and rare.

Afterwards they come to cozy quarters
To sit in comfort by the chimney corner,
Where servants serve them frequent stoups of wine,
And gaily they agree to do again
Tomorrow as they've managed it today:
Exchange whatever they achieve by chance
And as with it they meet at end of day.
They state assent before the full assemblage,
Seal it in high spirits with a toast,
At last politely take their goodnight leave
And each man hies to bed without delay.
The cock had hardly crowed and cackled thrice
As lord and lieges leapt up from their beds.
When meat and Mass were meetly meted out
They hurried to the woods ahead of day on
                              hunting bent.
               Hearty, men and horns
               Through morning meadows went.
               Unleashed among the thorns,
               The hounds picked up the scent.

They soon give tongue beside a marshy thicket.
The hunters urge those on that nose the scent first,
Driving them with shrill, excited sounds.
The other hounds that hear it hasten there
And forty of them hit the trail with fury.
Such a yap and yowl of yelping dogs
Arose, the rocks rang all around them with it.
Huntsmen heartened them with voice and horn
And all the pack together pushed between
A tarn and an intimidating crag.
A knoll beneath a cliff and near the marsh,
With boulders strewn about in bold confusion,
Brought their find. The hunters followed fast.
They cast about the crag and by the cliff,
The hunt aware their height kept in its hold
The beast the bloodhounds bayed by giving tongue.
They beat the bushes boldly then to start him,
And he in sudden fury seeks escape,
Lunging at the line of men in vain.
The boar whose brunt they bore there was a beauty,
A loner that had long since left the herd,
Grown, aggressive, greatest of all swine,
And when he grunted, grim; and then men groaned,
For three he thrust to earth at his first thrust
But did no further damage as he charged.
The hunters halloo Hi! and cry Hey! Hey!
Clap their horns to lips and sound recall.
Many are the mouths of hounds and men
That crowd the boar with cry and roar until the copse
                              resounds.
              He turns and stands at bay,
              Savaging the hounds,
              And piteously they
              Run howling at their wounds.

Archers come in haste to take their aim then,
Loose their arrows at him, hit him often,
But the heads are blunted by the brawn
Of skin and flesh that shields the boar's shoulders,
Nor can penetrate between the eyes;
The shaft may splinter with the powerful shooting,
Yet the head rebounds from where it hits.
But as their ceaseless strokes begin to sting him,
Fighting mad, he turns upon the men
And pricks them painfully at every plunge
Till many flinch before him and fall back.
But the lord, relentless on a light horse,
Blows his bugle, bent upon the chase,
Sounds the recall, rides through heavy brush
Pursuing this wild swine till nearly sunset.
And so with deeds like this they spend the day,
The while our handsome hero hugs his bed,
Our Gawain gay at home with gorgeous gear of
                                        every kind.
            The lady comes to wake him
            In manner quite refined,
            At once sets out to make him
            With reason change his mind.

She comes up to the curtain, peeps in quick;
At once Sir Gawain gaily says good morning.
Morning fresh, she makes her compliments,
Then smiling sits down softly by his side
And with a charming look she chides him thus:
"If you're Gawain, I regard as strange, sir,
One so well attuned to virtue always,
Cannot keep society's nice customs.
Should one try to teach you to attain them,
You cast them out completely from your conscience.
You forgot at once what yesterday
I taught you with the truest talk I know."
"What?" he asks. "I'm not aware of it.
If what you state is so, I blame myself."
"And still I taught you," says the lady, teasing,
"To kiss where form that's fair affirms you may."
"Unspeak your speech, my dear," that strong man answers,
"That I dare not do, it might undo me.
If she refused, I'd be a fool to offer."
"In faith," our fair one laughs, "no one'd refuse.
You're strong enough to force it, should that suit you,
If any were so ill-bred as deny it."
"By heaven," answers he, "your words are handsome,
But force is frowned on in the world I'm from,
As well as every gift not given gladly.
To kiss at your request's my charming duty;
But you may love or leave it, lady, when you like
                    and where."
            She leans in lovely fashion,
            Inclined to kiss him fair.
            They tell old tales of passion,
            Of joy and of despair.

"I wished some wisdom from you, wise sir," said
The noble lady, "nor were you annoyed;
So expert are you, and so young and eager,
So knightly and gallant you're known to be.
And as we see, respecting chivalry,
The choicest thing to choose from all the code's
The lovely game of love that leads a lover
To arms. For if we talk of trusty knights,
It is the text and title of their teachings
How lads for love have lived their lives in danger,
Suffered painful seasons for their sweetheart,
Avenged her wrong, reversed it by their valor,
Brought joy to her at home, so high their virtue.
You're this generation's gentleman,
Your fame and fine repute outfly your presence;
I've come to sit here twice within these curtains
But heard no single sound escape your lips
Owing anything at all to love.
And still you're so complaisant and gallant
You ought to take a young thing eagerly
And teach her tokens of the art of true love.
Why!—are you ignorant with all your fame?
Do I appear too poor a thing to profit from
                              your play?
                    For shame! Alone I sit here
                    To learn what lore I may.
                    Do demonstrate your wit, dear,
                    The while my lord's away."

Cries Gawain, "In good faith, may God repay you!
It's my proper pride and special pleasure
That one of such high worth would wish to come here
And try to entertain so tame a fellow
With any show of sufferance, so I'm charmed.
To take upon myself to teach of true love
And treat the themes in texts and tales of arms
With you, who wield more skill, I'm well aware,
In that fair art, by half, than I do now
Or ever shall, or any hundred others
Like me in this land are like to do,
Would, I feel, be foolish, fairest lady.
I'd wish that what you want would match my talents,
As I'm in happy duty held to serve you
And ever shall be, so the good Lord save me!"
Thus she tried him often, tempting him
To woo her, with whatever was her aim;
But his defense unfolded flawlessly.
Nor was there any wrong suggestion in their jests
                              as they
              Together laughed in glee.
              At last they said good day,
              Then kissed once more and she
              Softly went her way.

Then Gawain stirs himself, descends to Mass,
And shares the splendid dinner set before them.
Afterwards he whiles away the hours
With the ladies while his lordship gallops
Cock-a-hoop across the countryside,
Pursuing without stop that sainted swine,
Which stood at bay along the banks and at
Each bellow broke the lord's best brachets' backs,
Until the bowmen boldly broke it up
And made him move despite his might, as they
All came and caught him in a cloud of arrows.
And still at times he'd stop to strike, undaunted,
Until, exhausted, he could hardly run.
Desperate, at last he reached a crevice
In a rocky shelf beside the stream.
His back against the bank, he paws the ground,
The froth comes foaming fiercely from his mouth,
He grinds his gleaming tusks. This gives the huntsmen
Pause, though tired of tracking at safe distance as
                              they'd been.
            He's hurt so many of them
            By then they're no more keen
            To feel his keen tusks on them,
            Now he's trapped and mean;

Until their sire comes spurring up and sees
The boar at bay, the huntsmen all about him.
Leaping lightly down, he leaves his horse,
Pulls his bright blade out, strides boldly forward,
Splashes swiftly through the stream to where
Defiant stands his formidable foe.
The swine sees his assailant sword in hand,
His hair stands up, he snorts so angrily
That many think their man might meet his match.
The swine assaults the seignior straight away,
So man and beast are tumbled both together,
Buried in the water's boil. The beast
There met his master, for at their first meeting
The man had marked the slot below the throat
And now he rammed his blade directly in it
Right up to the hilt and hit the heart.
The swine conceded snarling, sliding instantly
                              beneath
                    The brook. The brachets claw him
                    And tear him with their teeth.
                    On dry ground where men draw him
                    The dogs do him to death.

Such thrilling trills of *prise* on many trumpets!
Such high halloos as loud as lads were able!
The brachets bayed the beast, obeying masters
Who'd led the hunt in that long-labored chase.
Then one acquainted with the woodsman's craft
Sets about the brittening of the boar:
First he hews his head off, hangs it up,
Then rends him roughly right along the back,
Brings the bowels out, on hot coals broils them,
Rewards the brachets with them mixed with bread.
He brittens off the brawn in broad white strips,
Then properly removes the inner morsels;
He ties the halves together whole and then
Hangs them firmly on a heavy pole.
Briskly now they bring the boar home,
The head in honor borne before the hero
Who'd conquered in the stream by strength of hands and
                                  sword arm there.
                    The lord can hardly wait
                    To reach the hall floor where
                    He calls our knight, elate,
                    Who comes to get his share.

The lord cries out aloud with merry laughter
And shouts in greater glee on seeing Gawain.
They get the ladies, gather up the household;
He shows the brawn to them and boasting tells
How large he was and long, how savage also
The war where in the woods the wild swine fled.
The knight appropriately praised his deeds,
Commending what he showed as of great merit;
For such a brawny beast, the bold knight said,
He'd never seen before, nor such great sides.
The hog's head then they handled and he praised it,
Feigning horror so the host could hear him.
The good lord cries, "Now Gawain, this game's yours
By word that's fixed and firm, as you know fully."
Says the knight, "That's true and it's as certain
That all I get in turn I give to you."
He caught the man about the neck and kissed him
And served him just the same a second time.
"Now we're even," laughed the knight, "this evening,
Keeping, since I've come here, all the covenants
                              we've made."
           "You're the best I've met,
             By Saint Giles," then said
             The lord. "You'll be rich yet,
             You drive so brisk a trade."

They put the tables up upon their trestles,
Covered them with cloths, then lights were kindled
Warm upon the walls from waxen torches.
In the hall the servants set the supper
And served it to the company assembled.
The din of merrymaking mounted merry
In many forms before the great hall fire;
At supper splendid songs were sung, and after,
Christmas chants and all the newest carols,
With mirth as mannerly as men might make it;
Our able hero by his lady ever.
She keeps up such a covert countenance,
But seemly still, to please her stalwart knight
That he's put off and angry with himself,
Yet may not for nice manners now deny her,
But turns her turns of phrase with turns, though they in turn
                                        are turned.
                        When they had had their fill
                        Then lord and guest adjourned
                        To where, in private, still
                        A cozy fire burned.

And there they drink and talk and think on New Year's
Eve to do as they have done today.
But Gawain asks to leave the morning after:
The moment's near to which he is committed.
The lord consents but seeks to make him stay
And says, "As I am sure, I swear to you,
You'll reach the Chapel ready for your business
On New Year's long, sir knight, before forenoon.
Therefore sleep upstairs and stay at ease
And I shall comb the copse and keep our compact,
Exchange what I achieve for your achievement;
For I have tried you twice and found you true.
Please remember then tomorrow morning,
'The third throw thrives the best'; so let's be thankful,
Make merry now and keep our minds on pleasure,
There's time enough to turn the tune to sorrow."
Gawain, granting this, agreed to stay.
Drinks were served them cheerfully, then servants brought
                    them light.
        Gawain went to bed,
        Slept sound and soft all night.
        The hunt still in his head,
        His lordship rose up bright.

After Mass his men and he had breakfast.
The morning glistened as he mounted gaily,
The hunters who should ride with him were waiting
Seated on their nags outside the gates.
The fields were fair, the frost still clinging to them;
Wreathed in red, the sun through cloud drifts rises
And sails above them shining in the sky.
Beside a wood the huntsmen freed the hounds,
The rocks rang round them with the ringing horns,
Some fell upon the scent where lurked the fox,
Tracking back and forth the twisting trail.
A kenet cries a find, the hunt acclaims him;
With rising sound the pack comes sniffing there,
Then rushes in a rabble on their quarry,
And he's away before them; soon they find him
And when they see him swiftly they pursue,
Denouncing him with angry indignation.
He twists and turns through many twisted thickets,
Doubles back, lies doggo neath the hedges.
At last he leapt a ditch along a fence
And stole out silent through a boggy wood,
Thinking with his wiles to worst the hounds,
But went, unwitting, to a waiting station,
Where greyhounds, three together, threatened, leaping at
                         their prey.
            He swiftly swerved again
            And streaked another way;
            Unhappy and in pain,
            To wood he went away.

'Twas heaven then to hear the hounds as they
Raised their cry when all had come together,
In chorus called such imprecations down
Upon his head that moment, as would make
The climbing cliffs come clattering down in heaps.
They halloo as the hunters come upon him,
They snarl at him and loudly shout their scorn,
They threaten him and often call him thief.
The trackers at his tail, he cannot tarry;
They rush at him whenever he runs out,
He turns back, twisting, Reynard is so tricky.
He leads them, strung out, lord and lieges both,
Over hill and dale all afternoon.
At home our hero's getting wholesome rest
Behind the cozy curtains that cold morning.
Love, though, would not let the lady sleep
Nor would the harm she harbored in her heart.
She rose up rapidly and went to him,
In a handsome robe that reached the floor
And warmly furred with fine furs finely felled,
No cover on her head but clear cut gems
Fixed upon a fret in full-set clusters,
Her lovely face and fair throat all uncovered,
Her soft breast and her shoulders bare as well.
She came within the chamber door and closed it
After her and swung a window open,
Called to him and taunted him with teasing words,
                    the dear,
          "Oh, man, how can you sleep,
            The morning is so clear?"
          In troubled trance sunk deep,
            He yet began to hear.

Wrapped in restless reverie he mumbled,
A man that morning tried by many fancies:
How destiny should deal his fate that day
When he saw the stranger at the Chapel
And stood the stroke he should without more talk;
But when she came, recovered consciousness,
Dragged himself from dreams at her address.
The lady, lovely, laughing, leaned to him,
Took his comely face and kissed him fair.
He greets her graciously with graceful welcome.
She seemed so glorious, so superbly dressed,
So faultless in her face, so fine her color,
That joy welled up and warmed his worried heart.
With fair and gentle smiles they fell to flirting
And all that lay between them was alluring, gay
                       and bright.
          They bandy words, half mean them,
          Indulging their delight.
          Great peril lay between them
          Should Mary fail her knight.

Because that precious princess pressed him so,
Nearly to the limit, he's obliged
To take her love or tactlessly refuse her.
His courtesy concerned him and he could not
Be a boor, but neither could he sin,
Betray a husband's hospitality.
"Forbid it, God," he begs, "it shall not be!"
He parried all her points with pleasant laughter,
The lovely speeches pretty on her lips.
She said to him, "You, sir, deserve rebuke,
Should you not love the lass you lie beside,
A lady wounded in her loving heart
Above all other women in the world,
Unless you love another lady better
And keep your faith to her so firmly fixed
You cannot let it go—and I believe that.
Tell me true, I beg, that this is so
And for the sake of other sweethearts do not say
                          with guile
            It's not." "Then by Saint John,"
            Our knight says with a smile,
          "I swear that I love none
              Nor will love for a while."

She says, "That word's the worst of all: I want
An open answer and I find it hurts.
Now kiss me prettily and I'll depart
For I who love too much may only mourn."
Sighing she reclined and kissed him sweetly,
Sat up softly, saying as she stood,
"Please pay me pleasure, dear one, as we part
And give me, say, your glove, as a memento,
A gift to me to make my mourning less."
"Quite willingly," he says, "I wish I'd with me
The finest thing on all the earth I own,
Because you ought to have by every right
An even greater gift than I can give.
A token hardly having any value
Would hardly do you honor at this time:
Gawain's glove accorded as a keepsake!
I'm on an errand in an unknown land,
A man alone, and have no men with me
To bear a bulky baggage stuffed with treasures.
The circumstance distresses me, dear lady—
Yet each must take things as they are for good and not
                    repine."
        "O man of rich resource,"
          Then said that lady fine,
        "Though I have none of yours,
          Yet you'll have one of mine."

A ring of ruddy gold in rich designs
She gave him, with a gleaming stone on top
That blazed with fiery brilliance like the sun;
'Twas worth a tidy sum, you may be certain.
He would not touch it, but instead he told her,
"I want, God knows, no gifts just now, fair lady;
I've none to offer you and none will take."
She urged him earnestly but he refused:
On his oath, he swore, he would not have it;
And she so sorry for it as she said,
"But if you can't accept my ring because
It's worth so much and you don't wish to be
Beholden to me, you shall have instead
My girdle, which will be a smaller gift."
She brightly took a belt that bound her waist,
Wrapped beneath her robe around her tunic:
It was green in grained silk trimmed with gold,
Embroidered finger's breadth about the hem;
And that she held out to our hero, asking,
Winsome, would he take it, though unworthy.
But he vows he'll every way avoid
Both gold and gilded keepsake till God's grace
Shall see him through his stern adventure there.
"And so, I pray you, do not be displeased,
But give your efforts over nor my graceless nays
              regret.
              For all you've done so kindly
              I'm dearly in your debt.
              In foul and fair you'll find me
              Your faithful servant yet."

"This silk as well, sir," says she, "you refuse,
  So simple in itself? It seems so surely,
  For look, it is so little and worth less.
  Yet one who knew the virtues woven in it
  Would value it, I vow, at higher value;
  For any knight who's girded with this green band,
  While he feels it firmly fixed about him,
  No hand under heaven here can hew him,
  For he may not be maimed by any means."
Our hero then rehearsed within his heart,
Thinking of his fate before the Chapel,
What a jewel this in jeopardy!
If, bending down, he bore his naked blow
And still survived it, that would be superb!
He suffered her to speak now; still beseeching,
She pressed the belt upon him, bade him wear it;
He granted and she gave it with good will.
She sought him for her sake to keep it secret,
Concealing it especially from her lord.
Our knight agreed that none should know indeed, but
                    only they.
          Full in heart and mind,
          He knew not what to say.
          And then that lady kind
          A third time kissed that day.

She lightly took her leave and left our hero,
Who had for her no further entertainment.
When she's gone, at once Sir Gawain's up,
Arrays himself in rich robed elegance,
Puts away with care his lover's keepsake,
Hiding it where handily he'll find it.
To the castle's chapel then he came,
Approached a priest in private, and he prayed him
To hear how he had lived and better lead him
To save his soul when he resumed his journey.
With fair intent he there confessed his faults,
His sins both great and small, and sought God's mercy
And asked for absolution of that man.
And he absolved and cleansed him so securely
The next day should have been the day of doom.
Afterwards he entertained the ladies,
Scintillating so with song and story,
High in spirits, as he'd seldom done there since
                    his stay.
            When daytime drew to night
            They felt it fair to say
            He'd never shone so bright
            As he had shone that day.

Now let's let him lie where love waylays him!
Leaping still across the land, his lordship
Seeks his kill with assiduity.
He's headed off the fox he's so long harried;
As he vaults a fence to view the villain
Where he hears the hounds come hurrying,
Through a rough grove, panting, runs Reynard
With all the rabble racing at his heels.
The man sees where he comes and waits there wary,
Brings his bright blade out and strikes at him.
The fox springs back and seeks to swerve away.
Rushing up, a hound, however, has him;
They fall on him before the horse's feet,
Worrying with wrath the wily wretch.
The lord alights at once and leaps among them,
Snatches him from out their savage jaws
And holding him above his head, halloos
Amid the howling chorus of the hounds.
The huntsmen hastened there, their horns all ringing,
Sounding recall till they saw the stragglers.
When the gallant crowd had come together
Those with bugles blew their blasts as one,
Those who lacked them lent their loud halloos.
Such merry music men have never heard!
The hymn they raised to Reynard's soul, it rang without
a crack.
The hounds have their reward,
Men pat and praise the pack,
Then rip from poor Reynard
The coat that clothes his back.

They ambled back then, night was almost on them,
Blowing bravely on their mighty bugles.
The lord alights, to his delight at last
Come home; a fire's heaped upon the hearth,
The good Sir Gawain standing gay beside it,
Playing love-or-leave-me with the ladies.
He wore a gown of blue that swept the ground;
His surcoat, softly furred, quite suited him,
His hood of matching stuff lay on his shoulders,
And coat and hood were each one trimmed in ermine.
He crossed the floor to meet his kindly host,
Greeted him and said in high good humor,
"Now this time I'll fulfill our treaty first,
  That happy deal we made and drank our drink to."
He takes the lord and three times kisses him—
Salutes as strong and stout as he can serve them.
"By Christ," then laughs the lord, "you're very lucky
  In your affairs, you've fully found a bargain."
"How good it is, no matter," quips Sir Gawain,
"Since I've plainly paid the price I owe."
"Mary," cries the other man, "mine's poorer,
  I've hunted all day long and only had
  This dreary fox—the Devil take his hide!
  That's pretty poor to pay for things so precious
As what you've cleanly dealt me, three such kisses, each
                        one good."
              " 'Twill do, thanks, on my word,"
                Cried Gawain, "by the rood!"
                Then how they slew Reynard
                The lord told as they stood.

With fun and tunes and all the food they fancied
They mightily amused themselves that evening,
Women laughing, witticisms winging,
Gawain and his good host very glad,
Except for cases where the company
Would do things to excess or drink too deeply.
Both these men made jests, and many others,
Until quite plain the hour approached for parting
And in the end they had to go to bed.
Our noble knight's the first to say good night,
To give his thanks and voice his gratitude:
"For such a happy stay here as I've had,
For hospitality this holy season,
May the Holy King on high repay you!
If I may have a man, then I'm your man, sir,
For as you know, I'm off tomorrow early;
Send a man to show me, as you said,
The road by which to reach that same Green Chapel
Where I must face the fate that's to befall me
As God may deal it out on New Year's Day."
The good host cries, "In good faith, I'll be glad
To pay the promise promptly that I made you,"
Assigns a squire to set him on the road
And lead him through the hills without delay
So he can go by grove and grass the way his goal
                          directs.
          Sir Gawain thanks the lord,
          Pays him his respects,
          Then with a parting word
          Forsakes the gentler sex.

He leaves the ladies, sad, with love and kisses,
Pressing on them pretty thanks in plenty;
They in turn return the like to him
And sighing soft, commend him to the Saviour.
Then he makes his manners and withdraws.
All the men he met upon the way
He thanked for service and each separate kindness
By which they'd all, with care, increased his comfort.
The servants, too, were sad to see him go,
Accustomed to his kind consideration.
Men with lights then led him up to bed,
Cheerful to his chamber, there to rest.
But was his slumber sound I dare not say,
For what should come tomorrow surely stirred and stirred
                    his thought.
          Let him lie there still,
          He's close to what he sought,
          And if you'll listen still
          I'll tell what fortune brought.

Part IV

Now comes the New Year near and night goes by,
The dawn drives out the dark, as Heaven demands.
Outside the winter's weather wakes, grows wild,
The clouds cast down their steely cold to earth—
Norther now enough to nip the naked!
The frosty snow descends on shivering beasts,
Loud the blast blows howling from on high
And piles the drifts up deeply in the dales.
Our hero listened long as he lay waking,
Kept his eyelids closed but could not sleep;
As each cock crowed he clearly caught the message.
With deft address he rose before the daybreak
By a lamp that lit his chamber's gloom;
He called his servant, who came quickly in,
And bade him bring his burnie and his saddle.
The servant rubs his eyes and finds the raiment,
Gets Sir Gawain groomed in all his gear:
First the hero's clothes against the cold
And then the fighting armor, freshly burnished,
The pauncer and the breastplates polished clean,
The burnie's rings abraded of their rust.
The groom has made them glisten, Gawain's gracious to
                          concede:
            He's rubbed them by the hour,
            Each piece with care indeed.
            Now knighthood's finest flower,
            Sir Gawain, summons his steed.

While getting ready in his richest raiment—
His vest in velvet bright with his device
Embroidered on it, set and bound with stones
Having special virtues, and the seams
Concealed with skill by sewn-on ornaments,
And finely furred inside with handsome furs—
He had not overlooked the lady's keepsake
Nor forgot she gave it for his good.
When he'd hung his sword upon his hip
He tied his token twice around him firmly;
Fixed about his waist it suited fine,
The silken girdle green, which sat so gay
Against the royal red on which it rested.
But Gawain did not bear it for its beauty,
For pleasure in its pretty shining pendants
Or the gold that glittered round the borders,
But to save himself when he should stand
And silent bend to sword or knife, the stroke should not
                                take long.
            He seeks the courtyard then,
            Accoutered rich and strong,
            And grateful, once again
            Salutes the noble throng.

Great and strong, good Gringolet stands waiting;
He's spent a happy stay, serenely stabled,
But spirited, he's ready for a run.
Our hero comes to him and rubs his coat,
Tells himself without exaggeration
And swears to them as well that on his word,
"This castle's constantly concerned with kindness.
May the master who maintains it and his men
Together get the joy of all their good,
The lady, too, be loved for all her life.
As they receive with such consideration
A stranger and so treat him with distinction,
May the Knight who holds high Heaven grant them,
And all of you, his honored recompense!
And if I live for long, you may believe me,
I'll seek you out some suitable reward."
He stands upon the stirrup, mounts his steed,
Receives his shield and slings it on his shoulder,
With his gilded spurs goads Gringolet,
Who springs upon the stones, no longer stopping now
                    to prance.
            The man then mounts his horse
            Who bears his spear and lance.
            Cries Gawain, "Bless this house,
            Send all in it *bonne chance!*"

The bridge was got down and the gates unbarred
And slowly swung wide open on both sides.
He thanked the men who moved them, crossed the moat,
Praised the porter kneeling in respect,
Who said, "Good day, Sir Gawain, God protect you";
And went upon his way with one man only,
The one to point him to that place of peril
Where he should receive the wretched stroke.
They rode by banks where all the boughs were bare,
They climbed across the cliffs where clung the cold.
The clouds, though moving high, were menacing,
Mist hung on the moors and soaked the mountains
And every hillside had a cloak of dew.
Brooks boiled up and burst across their banks,
Foaming on the fields they overflowed.
Through woods the way became bewildering
Until the time for sunrise should arrive that time
                    of year.
          They stand upon a height,
          The snow about them clear;
          The man beside the knight
          Says, "Sir, I beg, stop here.

"I have got you here this morning early;
 Now you're nearly at the noted spot
 Which you have sought and struggled so to reach.
 But let me tell you, since I've learned to know you
 And you're one living man whom I love much,
 You'll prosper better if you pay attention
 To my judgment, do as I suggest.
 The place toward which you're pushing's perilous.
 A dreadful creature dwells there in that desert,
 The worst one in the world, he is so wicked;
 He's strong and fierce and very fond of striking
 And mightier than any man on earth,
 His body bigger than the best four knights'
 In Arthur's house, or even Trojan Hector's.
 He's marked the Chapel his domain, so that
 None, however proud in arms, may pass
 Whom by a blow he does not do to death.
 For he's without restraint and shows no mercy;
 Come churl or chaplain riding by the Chapel,
 Monk or priest or any other man,
 He likes to kill as quick as he can catch him.
 As certain as you sit here in your saddle
 I tell you therefore, once you get down there
 You're finished if that fiend decides to do it.
 Trust me, sir, that's true, though you have twenty lives
                    to spare.
               He's long lived, Heaven knows,
               By brutal brawling there;
               His overwhelming blows
               Not even you can bear.

"Therefore leave the man alone, my lord,
  And for God's sake, go some other way!
  Select another land, may Jesus lead you,
  And I shall hie me home, and here I promise
  And swear by God and all his holy saints,
  So help me God and Heaven and on my honor!
  To keep your secret safe and never spread
  The story that you failed to face your foe."
"Obliged," the knight replied with plain displeasure,
  "I wish you well for what you'd do for me.
  However, though you kept your oath with honor,
  If I turned away and tried to flee
  Because of fear, in keeping with your counsel,
  I'd be a coward knight without excuse.
  Whatever shall ensue, I'll seek the Chapel
  And speak with that same man and say my say
  For weal or woe, no matter which, as fate may work
                    her will.
            Though the churl be grim
            And quick with club to kill,
            We yet can count on Him
            To save his servants still."

"Mary!" cries the man, "you make it plain
  You're bent on bringing harm upon yourself.
  And if you'd really like to lose your life
  I cannot see that I can keep you from it.
  Here's your helmet, put it on your head,
  And here's your spear, now take it in your hand,
  And ride the track down by that rock until
  It brings you to this tangled valley's bottom.
  Shortly to your left you'll see a glade
  And standing there the chapel that you seek,
  And find the fearsome fellow who defends it.
  Goodbye, noble Gawain, God go with you;
  I'd not go for all the gold on earth
  Nor walk beside you farther through this wood."
At that he twists the reins and with his heels
He hits his horse as hard as he can do it
And leaps away and leaves the knight within that
                              forest dim.
              "By God," says Gawain, "still
                  I'll sing no dirge or hymn;
                  Obedient to his will,
                  I put my trust in Him."

Then he pricks his steed and picks the path,
Slithers down the hillside by a shaw
And rides right through a rough patch to the dale.
He looked around, it looked all wild to him;
He saw no sign of shelter round about
But slopes set steep and high on either side
And rough and rugged crags of ragged stone,
Whose shaggy tops were skimmed by clouds, it seemed.
He halted and he held his horse in check,
Rode slowly back and forth to find the Chapel.
He sighted no such structure, which seemed strange,
But in a clearing, standing back a little,
What looked to him to be a tumulus,
A rounded mound that rose beside the borders
Of a stream that swiftly scurried by
And bubbled there as if the brook were boiling.
He pressed his horse ahead, approached the glade,
Alighted lightly, looped his noble courser's
Reins around the rough branch of a linden.
He went up to the barrow, walked about it,
Debating with himself what it might be.
It had a hole each side and on the end,
Was greatly overgrown with grass in clumps
And hollow inside. Just an ancient cave
Or crevice in a crag, he thinks, but can't tell if
                              he's right.
              "Is this that Chapel dear,
                  O Lord?" then cries our knight.
              "The Fiend might well say here
                  His matins in the night!"

"It's desolate," our hero cries, "indeed!
  This oratory's rank and overgrown;
  It well becomes the creature clad in green
  To do devotions here the Devil's way.
  I feel in my five senses it's the Fiend
  Himself who's set this meeting to destroy me.
  This is, sure, a chapel of disaster,
  May bad luck bring a bitter end upon it,
  The most accursèd church I've ever come to!"
With helmet on his head and lance in hand
He climbs the roof of this rough residence.
From that hill he heard, behind a rock
Across the stream, a high-pitched sound like someone
Sharpening a scythe upon a grindstone.
Grind! It rattled in the rocks as if to raze them!
Grind! It whirred and whined like water through a mill!
Grind! It shrilled and screamed to set the teeth on edge!
Says Gawain then, "By God, these goings-on
Are fixed up in my honor, my fine fellow, just to
                              greet me.
             But though I lose my head,
             As God works, when you meet me,
             I'll not now cry in dread,
             Mere noise will not defeat me."

106

Our knight then lifts his voice and calls out loud,
"Who rules this roost, who's ready to receive me?
For your good Gawain's got here in good time.
If someone's wanting something, let him hurry,
It's now or never, no time for neglect."
"Patience," cried the person overhead,
"You'll have whatever's owing soon enough,"
And went on with his whetting yet a while,
Would not descend till it was sharp to suit him.
He came across a crag and through a crevice,
Down a hollow, whirling his wild weapon,
A brand-new axe to pay his debit back;
Of Danish make, it had a massive bit
Curved to fit the haft and honed and huge,
A full four feet as figured by the thong;
The fellow all in green as formerly,
Face and figure, fall of locks and beard,
Except that now he walked the wild on foot.
Tapping on the stones as with a stick,
He strode, the haft beside him, to the stream.
He would not wade but went across it quickly,
Hopping with the hefty hatchet's handle.
Then grim he trod the snow aggressively,
Crossed the meadow's breadth to meet the man whom he
                            had heard.
            Our knight strides forward, meets him:
            To bow and scrape's absurd.
            "Good sir," the giant greets him,
            "I see you keep your word.

"God guard you, Gawain!" calls the man in green.
"You're really welcome to my residence;
  You've timed your travel as a true man should.
  You know by now the covenant between us:
  New Year's last you lent the loan allowed me
  And now I'm ready to arrange repayment.
  In this valley here we're all alone,
  No seconds, as we strike, may separate us.
  Take your helmet off and take your payment;
  Don't offer me more discourse than I offered
  When you whipped my head off at one whack."
"Nay, by God," cries Gawain, "as he grants,
  No grief will make me grudge one tiny grain.
  But strike a single stroke and I'll stand still
  And not resist your striking as it suits you, clean
                    and fair."
                  He bowed his neck then gravely,
                  Exposed his flesh all bare,
                  Holding himself bravely:
                  He dared not draw back there.

Then the green man gets himself all ready,
Takes the tool for Gawain's trial two-handed,
Heaves it up on high with all his sinews
As if he means to mar him mightily.
Had it driven down as deep as promised
Our doughty darling then were dead forever.
But Gawain, glancing sideways, glimpsed the axe
And as it swung down flashing to destroy him,
His shoulders shrank a little from its steel.
With a jerk the giant checks the blade,
Reproves the prince with proud and piercing scorn:
"You can't be Gawain, called the Great, who's never
Flinched in any field before a foe,
Yet flees for fear before he feels a tap!
I never heard such cowardice of him.
Nor did I flinch or flee when you obliged me
Nor spoil your aim in Arthur's house. My head,
Though to my feet it fell, I would not fall.
But you, your heart quails, having yet no harm!
So I'm the better man." Our hero heads off this
                    attack:
          "No more, one fault's enough,
            Though I have not your knack,
            For once my head is off
            I cannot put it back.

"But hurry, man, and have an end of it.
  Deal to me my destiny, and now,
  For I shall stand your stroke and shrink no more
  Until your axe has hit me, here's my word."
"Your head then!" shouts the other, lifts the axe,
  Standing stiff as if he were incensed.
  He takes a mighty cut but does not touch him,
  Holding back before it hurts. Our hero
  Takes it, all his limbs, without a twinge,
  But stands there like a stone, or rather stump,
  A hundred roots on rocky ground around it.
  Heartily the green man hails our hero:
"Your heart is whole and now it's right to hit you.
  Hold the honor high with which King Arthur
  Dubbed you. Save your neck if you can do it."
  Angrily our hero answers back,
"Well, strike away then, sir, if you're so steadfast.
  You threaten me with such a lot of talk
  That I've an inkling now your own heart's failing."
"You speak so sharp, for sure," the other shouts,
"There's no delay completing your affairs that I'll
                        allow,"
              Stands ready for the fray,
              Scowling, lips and brow;
              Nor is our hero gay:
              No hope for rescue now.

He lifts the axe up light and lets it fall,
The bit held straight to bite the neck laid bare.
But though he struck him sharp, still no great hurt:
He snicked him slantwise and so cut the skin;
The steel sank through the flesh and sent the blood
Spurting down the shoulders to the ground.
When Gawain saw the gore gleam on the snow,
He leaped ahead a lance length, legs together,
Got his helmet, put it on his head,
Set his shoulders safe behind his shield,
Brought his bright blade out and shouted bravely—
Never in the world was anyone,
Since his mother had him, half so happy—
"Stop your banging, bother me no more!
I've stood a blow, sir, here without resistance;
If you try another I'll return it,
I'll give you back as good as yours and you can count
                              on it.
            Just one stroke, that's all,
            By compact, you'll admit,
            Affirmed in Arthur's hall;
            So now, my good sir, quit."

The man refrained and rested on his axe,
Set the helve down, leaned upon the head
And gazed upon Sir Gawain in that glade,
How he stood there doughty and undaunted,
Fierce in arms; his heart went out to him,
And raising up a voice like rolling thunder,
He heartily addressed our heady hero:
"You needn't feel so fierce, sir, in this field.
No one here has used you ill or rudely
Or acted otherwise than as he owed you,
According to our vow in Arthur's court.
I promised you a blow, regard it paid;
Whatever claims remain, here's my release.
If I had been more agile, you'd have had
A knock that would have notably annoyed you.
The playful tap I tried first in pretense,
A cut that did not cut, I rightly claimed
Because that first night we affirmed our compact,
You swore your oath and honorably kept it,
That all you got you'd give me, like a good man.
The second stroke I struck you for the morning
You kissed my charming wife—you kissed me, too:
For both of these, the two pretended strokes I
                     offered here.
           When true man gives back true
           There is no harm to fear.
           The third time truth fell through
           And that tap cost more dear.

"For that woven girdle that you're wearing
  Is mine, my own wife wove it, I know well;
And I know well your kisses and your ways,
  The wooing by my wife—they're all my work.
I sent her there to tempt you and for certain
  I feel that you have proved as nearly faultless
As any man who ever walked the earth.
  As a pearl's more precious than a pea,
So is Gawain good above all good men.
  But here your loyal leanings lapsed a little,
Though not in skill at love or smooth good manners.
  You love your life, that's all; I hardly blame you."
Our sturdy hero stood a while bemused,
  Mortified and cringing in discomfort.
The blood rushed to his face and turned it red;
  The more the other spoke, the more he shrank,
Until the words burst wildly from his mouth:
"Cowardice and covetousness both
  I curse! In them reside the wrong and rudeness
That disrupt and ruin noble virtue."
  He took the twisted knot and he untied it
And grimly flung the girdle at the green man.
"There! For breaking trust, may bad luck take it!
  Anxiety about the stroke in prospect
Let cowardice persuade me to succumb
  To greed and so degrade my knightly nature,
Honor firm and generosity.
  I'm false and faulty, I who've always feared
Deceit and treachery: may sorrow seek them both,
                     and pain!
          I here confess, sir, still,
          My bad deed's now my bane;
          Once more grant your good will
          And I'll not fail again."

The other answered, laughing amiably,
"My injury I here consider healed.
You've made so fair confession of your failings,
Borne the open penance of my axe,
I hold you cleansed and cleanly purified
As if you'd never been at fault since birth.
I give you, sir, my girdle, edged in gold
And green as is my gown. My dear Sir Gawain,
Keep in mind this moment as you move
Among the proud and princely, and please take
This perfect token of a thing that passed
Between two gallant knights at this Green Chapel.
Then on this holiday you'll come home with me
And there, with revels, see the remnant of the
                              season go."
              The lord exhorts him then,
              Says, "With my wife, I know,
              You'll soon be friends again,
              Who once was your fair foe."

"No indeed," the prince replies, politely
  Takes his helmet off and thanks the man.
"For I have lingered long enough. Good luck,
  The Lord of honors rain down honors on you!
  Commend me to your courteous wife, she's charming,
  And to the other, both my honored ladies,
  Who so beguiled with grace their guileless knight.
  But it's no marvel men are made such fools of,
  Through women's wiles are brought to care and woe.
  For Adam was deceived by one himself,
  Solomon by many, and take Samson—
  Delilah did him in—and then there's David,
  Dazzled by Bathsheba, suffered for it.
  Women's wiles brought each one to disaster.
  'Twould be a triumph then if men could learn
  How to love and never to believe them.
  For these were men the mightiest of old
  Who hankered after happiness above all men
                              who dared,
                And they were all betrayed
                By those for whom they cared;
                And I too, I'm afraid,
                So may I, please, be spared?

"For your girdle," says he, "God repay you!
  While my will may work as I would wish,
  Not its shining gold or needlework,
  The silk or splendid pendants on its sides,
  The comfort or regard that it may get me,
  But the sin it signals, I shall see there
  As I look upon it long and often,
  Riding out to follow knightly fame,
  Renew in me remorse for this transgression,
  Remind myself: the faintness of the flesh,
  How it's ready prone to wrong enticement.
  Thus when pride shall prod me at my prowess
  One look then shall make my heart grow humble.
  But one thing would I beg, if you won't mind,
  Since you're the lord of that land where I lived
  With honor at your hands—may he reward you
  Who holds the heavens up and sits on high—
  Please name your proper name—and nothing more."
"That I'll tell you truly," says the other,
"Bertilak de Hautdesert, believe me,
  Is what the people call me in this country.
  Through Morgan's might, le Fay, who stays with me—
  Skilled she is in occult craft and cunning
  And in the many magic arts of Merlin,
  For formerly she had a love affair
  With that noted wizard who knows all your knights
                    by name;
              And so the goddess Morgan
              Is what we call that dame:
              The proudest princes she can
              Bring down and make quite tame—

116

"She got me, thus disguised through her great power,
To your pleasant hall to try the pride—
Was it real indeed?—on which now rests
The reputation of the Table Round.
She worked this wonder just to scare you witless
And drive your dear Queen Gaynor half to death
With gaping at a guest who like a ghost
Harangued the royal table, head in hand.
It's she there in my home, the ancient dame,
Your aunt indeed, half sister to King Arthur,
Daughter of the Duchess of Tintagel,
On whom afterwards great Uther fathered
Arthur, who is now held in such honor.
Hence I urge you, sir, to see your aunt,
Make merry in my house; my household love you,
And I wish you, on my oath, as well
As any, under God, for your high truth."
But no, the knight regrets, he'll not now do it.
The two men then embrace, entrust each other
To the Prince of Paradise and part there in
                              the cold.
            Back to Arthur's ground
            Goes Gawain riding bold;
            The knight in green turns round
            And hastens to his hold.

Alive by grace of God, on Gringolet
Sir Gawain rode the wild ways of the world.
He sometimes slept in houses, outdoors often,
Had adventures by the way and won,
But here I'll not repeat them for the present.
The wound upon his neck had also healed
And so he bore the bright green belt about it,
Slantwise like a baldric down his side,
Knotted neatly underneath the left arm,
To symbolize the spot that he was stained with.
And thus he came to court, our knight, intact.
High excitement rose within that house
When all the great folk heard that good Sir Gawain
Had arrived at home; it made them happy.
The king then kissed our hero, and the queen,
And many others came to do him honor
And ask him what had happened, and he told them,
Rehearsed the many hardships that he had,
What happened at the Chapel and the artful
Conduct of the knight, the lady's courtship,
In the end told how he had the girdle.
The nick he showed them on his naked neck
That he had suffered for deceit and so had stained
     his fame.
   As he spoke, it pained him,
   He groaned for grief and blame,
   The blood rushed up and stained him,
   As he confessed, in shame.

"Lo, lord!" the knight laments and lifts the lace,
"This band about my neck betrays the blame
  I bear, the damage that I've done myself
  Through cowardice and covetousness there,
  The token of the treachery I'm caught in,
  And I must wear it all my waking days.
  We cannot set ourselves, though we conceal it,
  Free from any fault that once we feel,
  For where it's fastened, there it's fixed forever."
The king gave Gawain comfort, but the courtiers
Laughed aloud at this, at once allowed,
These loyal lords and ladies of the Table,
That all the brotherhood should bear a baldric,
A band about them slantwise of bright green,
And wear it like our knight for love of him.
The Round Table's fame affects that fashion
And he who has one honors it forever—
As borne out by the best book of romances.
And so in Arthur's age this story happened,
Which the Brute Books all have brought to witness,
Since Brutus boldly brought us here at first,
Once the siege of Troy had ceased, nor did he choose
                              amiss.
              And many myths were born
              Before such feats as this.
              May he they crowned with thorn
              Please bring us to his bliss.
                              Amen.

And for our story's colophon we find:
Honi soyt qui mal pence, or Englished,
For shame, for shame, good sir, such shameful thoughts!
                    Amen, say I.

Christmas 1974

Library of Congress Cataloging in Publication Data

Gawain and the Grene Knight.
    Sir Gawain and the Green Knight.

    I.   Silverstein, Theodore, tr.
PR2065.G3   1974b   821'.1   74–17011
ISBN 0–226-75763-3